# Letters To

## JADE

ISBN:9781707880768

## DEDICATION

"You'll Be In My Heart, from this day on, now and forever more"
Phill Collins
Daddy, Sabrina and Aunt Cindy

Hi Beautiful Souls,

If you have found yourself with this book in the palm of your hands, then I assure you there is a reason. There is no specific order to these thoughts that I have touched pen to paper with, over the course of 5 years. Each feeling, moment, word, energy and emotion has been birthed from a place of healing, celebrating, mourning and really just living. I can only hope that my words reach you in a way that you have never felt before, that they reach out and give your heart a little squeeze as to let you know you are not alone. I left blank pages for you too. I encourage you to fill it with your magic.

I Love You,

Jade

@Jadenoelleviggiano

Peace is acknowledging the missing pieces without feeling empty

It is what we can endure that defines who we are and what we become, not our past.

# I AM LOVED

I wonder how many of us settle. How many of us just let the comfort of where we are stand in the way of what we truly want. I'm sure you have been there before, had the urge to say fuck it and take the leap but instead you wind up staying exactly where you are. We should leap more. Life is so short and so big. We have so much to do. We should start living more, saying yes more, saying 'F NO" to more things that don't serve us. Maybe if we start living while we are alive, we will start to realize what we truly want isn't so far fetched. Nothing is impossible.

I hope you make sure whatever it is you're doing is good for your soul.If you have the smallest inkling that it's not, then its not for you. The love that feeds you should feel satisfying, not leave you hungry.

# I AM WORTHY

We meet people at different stages in our lives. Some come and some go. Some lessons and some blessings. You walked in to my life at exactly the right time. Everything just fell into place from the moment you got close enough to me that I could almost hear your heart beat. This was the moment I knew that my life was going to change forever. Your movements, calm but bold, your face beautifully aligned and your voice clinging to my skin like soft silk. Mix it all together and here you have a soul so powerful and magnetic, so sweet but strong that has started a forest fire inside of me. Human touch has always been such a necessity in my existence and I realize now as I lay in bed, skin to sheets, eyes heavy and air cool that the human touch I melt for is yours. The butterflies in my belly and goosebumps that fall across my skin both as natural as the way your lips utter the words I love you. Three words so complex yet so simply true. We pray for these moments as little girls, day dream for them even and here we are. This is real, this is the fantasy side of reality and this is who you are, a mix of laughter, love and a safe place to land and from the way I am falling there is no better place I know than to land in your presence.

When you start to love yourself more you set yourself free from those who made you believe you were hard to love.

# I AM STRONG

Enough chasing. You and those meant for you shall run towards each other fiercely, until you feel your worlds collide.

The people that make you lose sight of who you are or question your worth are not the people for you.

# I AM FEARLESS

I found a broken seashell this evening. For a moment I held all the pieces in my hand, almost putting it back together, but then I stopped and let them fall into the sand, just as they were. I admired the edges and the faded colors, the lines and the chips. I realize now these pieces have weathered storms and tides and animals trying to pick at them. Through all of this, this one time whole seashell became parts. Parts of a story and these parts I've realized, these rough edges don't need to be put back together. They are abstract and different because of their imperfections. This is how they will stay and for that they are imperfectly beautiful. People are like that too.

Those face down in the dirt eat shit moments. Those moments don't hold a candle to the after math. The after math where you get up chin up eyes ahead and you make it through. THATS your defining moment. That's the moment that changes you. The moment you realize you got back up. You're getting there. We all are.

# I AM HOPEFUL

The way the storm approaches so naturally and takes full control of where it lands, the way it dangles anticipation in the grey sky over our heads, teasing us making us look it's way..leaving us begging for the rain to start and watch the way it leaves change among us, without a second thought, some embrace, some dance and some hide under the covers to its confident persona. A storm is free and it is unapologetically wild, never apologizes for being so intense or too much. I believe some of us were born to be a storm...Leaving our marks wherever we go.

We are a mess of wrongs trying to be right. Bruised and broken hearts that feel sore from the blows. Two souls melted together by the fire that tore them apart. Here we stand dazed and confused among the many thoughts that dance inside our heads like sunbeams that burn holes through our skulls. The sun with such beauty can burn you so deeply. You ask it: why must you burn me? I lean on you for warmth. The sun replies "oh honey anything warm and flowing that pulls you in is bound to burn you"

# I AM HEALTHY

Time doesn't care about how we feel or if we want it to slow down or pause or speed up. Time just ticks and expects us to move with it regardless of how we feel. The only way to beat time I always say...is to use it. So this is me telling you that you need to do just that. Use. Time.Life wants that. Use it beautifully, wildly smart and preciously because in the end it's all we have. We are incredible humans and those who we have lost are still a huge chunk of who we are. Energy never fades. Love never dies. It lives on within us. Remember that. I love you.

The way your eyes lay piercing across your face outshines the sun and the stars to follow. And your hands tell stories of hard work intertwined with deep love. Your shell like a canvas and your soul the paint swirling color after color designing all things beautiful. Beautiful like the moon who without a single word shines down on every person and every creature of the night silently screaming you are safe under my light. That is you. The moon. I believed it would take me years to understand what it felt like to feel whole from someone else and then like breath taken away at the sight of a sunrise you crossed my mind my path and my body. I may be sunshine but i am darker than nightfall and the only thing that seems to fit naturally in my darkness is you. The moon.

# I AM IMPORTANT

Maybe one day this will help

Maybe one day you'll read this and smile and realize how far you have come.

I believe in you...

I believe in you like the sun believes in the moon.

I believe in you like the sand believes in the ocean and the night believes in the morning. You are the surest thing I've ever felt in my bones and in my soul. Through thick and thin, high and low, up and down and inside and out I won't ever stop believing in you. Your life path is paved with bravery and courage. What you can not see right now you will see ten times closer and bigger when the time is right. All you are and all you do has kept my heart beating and my breath steady. Hand in hand and heart to heart every moment I will stand by you. Kiss your bumps and kiss your bruises. Every ending is a new beginning but we just don't know it at the time. Every failure is a bigger triumph but we don't see it until we are there. You are my love and sweet steady rock and I will be yours when you feel shaky. Whenever you need someone I will be there. If you just need someone to lay with you. I will be there. Simply to love and adore you. I will be there. To kiss your face and rub your chest. I will be there. To not say a word but give you one simple look of security. I will be there. To tell you this is going to always and forever get better. I WILL be there. You will always have me..

We all love the pretty parts don't we? The easy parts and the effortless ones as well. Where we smile and blow kisses and compliments. But what about when you're so far down that your face is flat on the floor and no matter what or who is in your way you are going to cry and scream at them? Who's there for you then? You want to know the easiest way to tell who will be a forever friend and who is genuine? Come undone in front of them. Show them your sad side, your dark side, your unapologetic side. If they grab your hand and say hey kick and scream at me all you want I'm still going to be there to help you find the light....you have found the right person(s). If they back away and choose you only in your prime and when you have no troubles to put on their shoulders cause the weights too heavy for you in this moment then it's time to walk away. You take all of me or nothing at all.

# I AM ABUNDANT

My strength didn't just show up one day. It took storms and bruises and a whole lot of struggle. It took tears and sadness and anger to show me just how strong I am. How capable I am of getting through things.

The time is now for trial and error.
The time is now for messy love.
The time is now for champagne on a Sunday and smoothies on a Monday.
The time is now to move until you feel the IT you're looking for.
The time is now to empower.

Now we take the lead with our hearts open for opportunity and beating for dreams brought to life.
Now we face our fears and feel them out until they turn to freedom.

Welcome to the next chapter, the shift is so real.
We have been waiting for you.

# I AM RESILIENT

Let's  connect to each other.

Let's go on a Judgement Detox.

Let's laugh a whole lot.

Let's cry it out too.

I think most of all...

Let's start believing we are worthy of love.

Giving it and getting it in return.

Trust it.

Your art work, body work, mind work, hard work, creative work and the process. It's okay to remove yourself and start over.
It's okay to dive in deep with those around you. Work is work.
If you do the work, no matter what it is, you will get the result
BUT...
Only if you trust in it's process.

# I AM PEACEFUL

Change opens the door...
Challenge pushes you through it.

If the seasons are allowed to change...

So are we.

# I AM UNDERSTANDING

.

.

What will it take for you to realize that you have a power unlike any other? Do you know the love that flows through your veins? Or how about the heart that beats in your chest?

You are more than alive, you are living.

I want us to wake up feeling free, knowing that this world is ours for the taking. Every single day we rise is a new start, new story, new beginning.

How cool is that?

We get this chance to rest too. We sleep off the past and awake in the present. Let's keep remembering this...

Tomorrow morning, we press...

Play.

# I AM LOYAL

Today is the day you decide to feel good inside and out.
The day you make the decision to wake up a little earlier, sit quiet for a few moments, let your inner guide take you on your journey to find what you truly want of this new day.

Repeat x 3

"I am mine before I am anyone else's" is such a super power mantra.

Self love first, baby.

# I AM PASSIONATE

When you are able to feel how you want without apologizing, that gives you a sense of happiness. That gives you a sense of freedom to feel happy.

:)

SELF LOVE GROCERY LIST:

Eat well
Love hard
Listen more
Speak kinder
Breath deeper
Show up
STOP complicating things for yourself

# I AM CONFIDENT

Home.

Home to me is a gut feeling. A beach around 5pm in early September.

It's me in my backyard at 9 years old playing basketball with dirty shoeless feet.

Home.

Home is my daddy watching me drive my toy car up and down the driveway and it is going with him to the home improvement store.

Home.

Home is the love of my life's yawn driving home from a long road trip.

Home.

Home is my best friends laugh.

Home.

Home is not a shell but what's inside.

Home to me is the creation of all the memories and feelings keeping me

alive.

If you're stuck in a rut...

Life is about facing it till you make it, not faking it till you make it.
Give yourself full permission to face the human in you. That will set you free
and move you forward in the constant direction of your beautiful future.

# I AM UNIQUE

Sometimes we go through a day just using our minds, but we need to remember what's constantly tapping at our chests.


Heart.

Think of where you were last year. Look at where you are now and how far you've come. You started to climb the mountain instead of continue to carry it on your gentle back. Look at yourself in the mirror, hold the stare long enough to feel proud of that human staring back.

# I AM CREATIVE

A Letter To The Messy You,

Life is tricky sometimes you know? You go through periods of time where everything fits like a puzzle, where you're at peace and you just know the next step is going to be as beautiful as the last one and then there are times where you're confused, where there are clouds more than there is sun, where the people and places you once knew felt like strangers.

You go through shit you know? You also grow through shit and yeah you lose yourself for a little while and you experience people and situations and emotions ...you do things...you fall down, you get back up, you live and you learn. So much goes on through it all but you try her and you love hard and you cry hard while you wonder how on earth you'll ever get off the rollercoaster and find calm waters again.

I think we can all relate to that I think we can all say that we've been in a place in our lives where we weren't sure what's going to come next and that has made us feel lost and just start to go through the motions and you pray or at least I do...I pray a lot...for clarity during the mess I had prayed a lot for clarity and I realized something along the twist and the turns, through the ups and the downs...

The ones who love us never really leave us and that your "meant to be" or that missing puzzle piece will find its way to you...

When you decide to give yourself the chance to love yourself again and be loved again.

Experience.

If you don't, you will never know
If you never know, you will always wonder...

I AM BLESSED

"The pain will fade" they tell me but I fear it won't. Even the smallest things are the biggest because I do not love small and I do not feel things small. It is who I am. I know the person you are supposed to be with through blood, sweat and tears will keep you and turn you fear into fuel to aid in your moving forward. If this person does not..think...think for a moment..If they cannot fight for you and love you through your seasons...are they worth it? No. Trust me you will know through the nights on the floor whose hand is their to help lift you up.

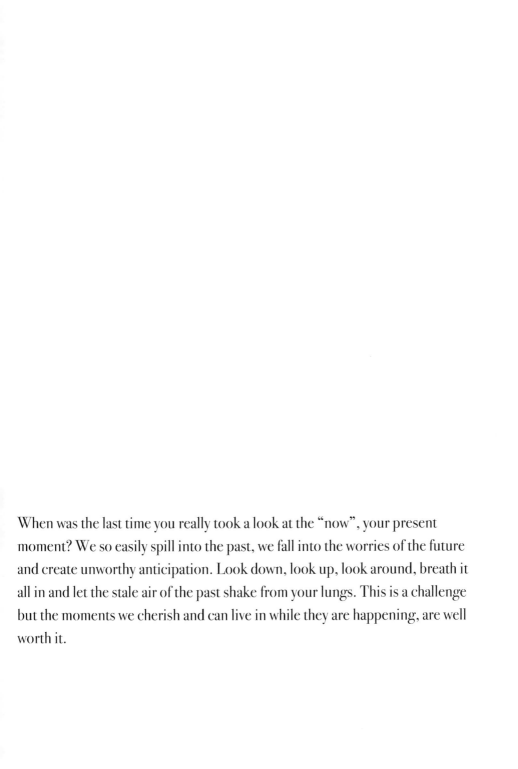

When was the last time you really took a look at the "now", your present moment? We so easily spill into the past, we fall into the worries of the future and create unworthy anticipation. Look down, look up, look around, breath it all in and let the stale air of the past shake from your lungs. This is a challenge but the moments we cherish and can live in while they are happening, are well worth it.

# I AM HARD-WORKING

Living fully and directly in an experience is the only truth we can claim. The only way we really know anything at all is through direct experience. Turn your check to the small voice in your head lead by your cruel ego, move away from the stories that appear in your brain based on past experience, trauma and triggers from the world we lived in as little boys and girls. Nothing in this life is real until you are actually IN it.

If we found ourselves in opportunity to sit down face to face with our younger years, maybe we would be brave enough to tell that child that everything they are feeling, going through, discrediting and running away from actually helped mold us into the human we are today.

# I AM WISE

I know how hard it may be to indulge in self worth or love. I know that it takes mountains to climb, knees to skin, hearts to break and even rejection to learn where all the power comes from. That's okay. It's all okay. It's all okay because one day you'll be given opportunity to face the mirror and realize it's been you the whole time. You that climbs the mountain, heals the knee, grows out of heart break and dances into the fire of success from the fuel of rejection. Always you who makes the changes into growth.

Time..

Time to think,
time to process,
time to let the tears fall,
time to learn,
time to love,
time to laugh,
time to feel and
time to heal.
I will never understand the way loss works but will always understand the way
love works. How it is eternal. How we can carry it with us day in and day out.
Something we can't see but oh boy can we feel it. I will continue to question
certain decisions the universe makes but I will never question the miracles that
come after. Kiss the people you love, rebuild bridges don't burn them, make
plans and follow through, say you're sorry, call, write, talk, make eye contact
and don't apologize for who you are. I urge you all...I love you all. Say I love
you more. We all need it..
We all damn need it.

# I AM GRATEFUL

It's so important...so important to recognize that, what we allow will continue. Allow yourself to knowingly love through all your confusion, to love the skeletons in your closet, love your damn messiness, love your scars, your perfections, imperfections, YOURSELF and love intimately and passionately at all times, without one damn regret, the person that YOU and your heart choose. Love is love and it is the ONE THING that outlives us all.

Take me to the magic place of leaves and trees and cracking branches beneath my feet. Where the world smells like a fireplace and feels like freedom. The hate in this world is getting to me. The unsafe after thoughts and sadness that weighs in my heart too. It's not just about putting a hashtag and praying for whatever has occurred on Social Media. It's about taking action. We need to take f*king action.

# I AM ENOUGH

For the "me toos", the ugly cry's, the screams, the I can't do this anymore, the runaways, the tears and snot wiping on your shirt sleeve, the drunk mistakes, the 3ams, the running thoughts, the breaking hearts and scars and bruises and bumps. You're still here. You have made it this far. You have a story to share and a life to live. I'll see you at the end of the tunnel where the light will be. I love you.

Just keep doing what you are doing and good things will happen.

# I AM POSITIVE

Despite the chaos, I find peace knowing my perspective and my personal growth are controlled by ME. That is where the success makes a home, in that knowing space. We deserve nothing. We earn it. Inspiration is everywhere and the shitty times are here to fuel your fire. Don't forget that.

Take me back to the times when all we ever cried over were skinned knees and getting picked last in dodgeball...

# I AM PRESENT

We were happy then...
A time in between day and night where the sun stayed low and the air was cool.
We never thought about the "what if's" of the future, just turned our cheeks to
the ticking clock and let our bodies dance heart to beating heart. I knew the
possibility of you breaking my heart, of course but I brushed it away like a
buzzing mosquito because my inner child wanted to believe you were here to
save me. Now months have passed and here we stand. You there and me here.
You're not saving me...

I'm saving me.

Like tiny fireflies lighting up the sky, your eyes they shined. Every time you spoke about something you loved, every time you'd tell me a story of the past, a happy memory, there it was…that light. The moment in time where the darkest of nights didn't feel so dark. You gave me hope. I've looked into so many eyes though, they'll never be yours but it's okay because every time i look at the night sky and the fireflies are dancing around, blinking and shining…I know it's you. I know you are here.

.

# I AM CONSISTENT

Organic Destiny: Souls come into, return, open and seep through your life for a myriad of reasons. Let them be who and what they are meant to. Do not force, push or pull a situation to what you think you want it to be. In the end, it is not about what you want, it is about what you need.

.

.

Maybe it has been the summer heat getting to my head, it could be that. It could be staying up on the roof with you until 3am thinking about all those silly little things in the past we would do. Remember how we would chalk the sidewalk, walk to the ice cream shop, walk back with a half melted vanilla cone in my hand, chocolate in yours. What I remember most though was the first time you ever touched me. You grabbed my shoulders that night and pushed me off the dock into the water. You stood behind me hands on my skin...I will never forget the way they felt. Now we are up here on my roof 3am, those hands on the brown slates and my back against the window to my room. Not a single touch felt. All I can think about as we sit here in silence are your hands, my shoulders, that dock. I wanna go back...

.
.

# I AM DRIVEN

My Wishes For You

I wish you the warmth of the sun upon your face each morning and a soft breeze to follow.
I wish you hammocks and bare-feet set to the tune of Hotel California
I wish you pizza that doesn't burn your mouth and beer with not too much foam.
I wish you endless conversation with someone you love on a roof, mountain, middle of the street at 3am, backseat of a car or wet sand and a dark ocean.
I wish you love that you only read about in history books.
I wish you time that stops when you're dancing in a dark room to your favorite song.

and most of all...

I wish you the courage to not only know your worth but to believe in it as much as I do.

.

.

"You won't forget me will you?" I said under my breath, as I walked away from the mirror.

To the girl whose messy hair, bruised heart and wild tear stained face taught me so many beautiful lessons...

Thank You.

.
.

# I AM ME.

Made in the USA
Coppell, TX
04 December 2019

11984975R00049